QUESTION BANK
ON
INTRODUCTION TO GRAPHICS

PREFACE

Graphics is a practical and one of the most fascinating subjects amongst youth. However, students find it difficult to answer theoretical questions when asked. They generally fail to express and reproduce theoretical knowledge required for Graphics and Designing. Introduction of Graphics in Primary and Secondary education has marked the importance of this subject. I have tried to provide a solution to this problem of theoretical questions in this subject. As an educator, students always asked me about the kind of questions they will be facing during exams and are there any question banks or reference books which can help them out. This book is an attempt to solve this problem and provide a question bank for exams and act as reference for interviews where theoretical knowledge holds equal importance.

I have referred syllabus of Savitribai Phule Pune University (Formerly known as Pune University), Gujarat University, Karnataka State Open University, Dr. Babasaheb Ambedkar Open University, Ajeenkya D Y Patil University, Poornima University, Sharda University, Yashwantrao Chavan Maharashtra Open University, Jain University before creating this book.

This book covers questions relating to Graphic Designing, Illustrations and related subjects. Utmost care has been taken to include all the major topics related to Photoshop and Illustrator.

Prof. Ankit Jain
Assistant Professor
Suryadatta Group of Institutes
B.Com (CA), MBA (Finance), AD3D+

ACKNOWLEDGEMENTS

Firstly, I would like to thank my parents, my younger brother and my beloved daughter for their uncompromised love and care. Their well wishes and wholehearted support cannot be acknowledged with words. This is a tiny attempt to thank them for encouraging me for writing this book.

I would like to thanks to Prof. Dr. Sanjay B. Chordiya, Founder President and Chairman of Suryadatta Group of Institutes for his continuous guidance, support and encouragement.

I would like to express my gratitude towards my friends who have extended their best wishes and have encouraged me to write this book. I would like to thank Dr. Gopal S Jahagirdar for inspiring me to write and Dr. Anand G Gaikwad for his able guidance. I would like to thank all my colleagues for their support and encouragement. It is bit difficult to mention everyone here but, I thank everyone who have helped, supported, encouraged and guided me directly and indirectly for writing this book.

I would also like to thank all my students for asking me a lot of questions and queries, in various ways, which motivated me to write this Question Bank on Introduction to Graphics.

Finally, I would like to thank and express my gratitude towards my better half, Mrs. Nishita Jain, for her support and encouragement in writing this book. Without her support this book would not have been possible.

I would also like to mention that a lot of effort has been taken to complete this book without errors; yet if readers find any lacking in some aspects, please consider it a human error and forgive me by providing their valuable suggestions for implementation in the further editions. I would also request readers to kindly provide their valuable feedback on this book.

With best wishes,

Prof. Ankit Jain

Assistant Professor

Suryadatta Group of Institutes

B.Com (CA), MBA (Finance), AD3D+, MESC

SYLLABUS COVERED

Course Title	Introduction to Graphics
Software	Photoshop & Illustrator

Unit	Contents
1	**Workspace – Photoshop** Workspace basic, Palettes and Menus, Toolbar – selection tools, painting tools, editing and retouching tools, zoom tools; Viewing images, Ruler, Guide and Grids.
2	**Preferences** Recovery and undo, Memory and Performance, Photoshop Images, Image size and Resolution, High dynamic range images.
3	**Colors** About color, Color modes, Converting between color modes
4	**Introduction to Menus** File, Edit, Image, View
5	**Selecting** Making selections, Adjusting pixel selections, Moving and copying selected pixels, Deleting and extracting objects, Saving selections and using masks
6	**Introduction to Menu – Layer** Layers, Selecting, grouping, and linking layers, Moving, stacking, and locking layers, Managing layers, Setting opacity and blending, Layer effects and styles, Adjustment and fill layers, Masking layers, Introduction to Channels
7	**Making color and tonal adjustments** Viewing histograms and pixel values, Understanding color adjustments, Adjusting image color and tone
8	**Introduction to Types** Different Types Tools, Character Panel, Paragraph
9	**Menu – Filters** Introduction to Filter basics, Filter effect, Applying specific filters, Add Lighting Effects, Liquify filter, Vanishing Point, Create panoramic images
10	**Automating tasks** Automating with actions, Creating actions, Processing a batch of files, Scripting
11	**Introduction to Adobe Illustrator** Illustrator is a sophisticated vector drawing tools.
12	**Introduction to new document** Selection tool, Group selection, Selection lassos, Magic wand selection, The Pen Tools, Convert anchor point
13	**Layers and Grouping** Layers introduction, Organizing layers, Selecting layers, Grouping layers, Group selection, Duplicating layers, Sub-layers, Collect and flatten, Creating templates, Placing paths
14	**Introduction to the Stroke** The Stroke, Stroke basics, Capitals and joining, The dashed line, Scaling strokes
15	**Introduction to Type** The type tool, Area type tool, Path type, Vertical type tool, Block text, Rows and columns, Wrap text, Missing font, Creating outlines, Spell checking, Font attributes, Character palette, Formatting paragraphs, Type transformation

16	**Introduction to Shape Objects** Rectangle tool, Rounded rectangle tool, Ellipse tool, Polygon tool, Star tool, Flare tool, The spaz modifier, Transformations
17	**Scale tool** Scaling patterns, Rotation tool, Rotating a pattern, Reflect tool, Twist tool, sheer tool, Reshape tool, Re-positioning art, Aligning and Distributing, object alignment, Mouse directed movement, Line Tools, line segment tool, Arc tool, Spiral tool, Rectangular grid tool, Polar grid tool, Spaz line tool, Moving lines, Compound Path and Clipping Mask
18	**Clipping masks** Clipping paths, Applying Color, Color introduction, Adobe color picker, Color palette, Swatches palette, Color picker theft, The Pencil Tools, Basic pencil tool, Smooth tool, Eraser tool
19	**The Brush Tool** Paintbrush introduction, Calligraphic brush, Art brush, Pattern brush, Loading and saving brushes
20	**Gradients** Gradients introduction, Editing gradients, Gradient libraries, Transparency and Masking, Object opacity, Targeted transparency, Transparency clipping, masking, knockout group, Blending modes, Enveloping and Meshes, Envelope introduction, using the warp, the mesh, Utilizing the top object, text distortions, Smart Guides and Rulers, rulers introduction, Creating guides, smart guides, extruding text, smart guide, options, grids, Measure and info tools, Scissor and Knife, the scissor tool, the knife tool
21	**Liquefy** Liquefy tools, More lignifications, Appearance and Styles, Styles introduction, Multiple strokes and fills, Converting effect to shape, Group appearance, The text bug, Distort and transform, Offset path effect, Pathfinder effects, Rasterizing, Document rasterization, Stylize effects, Pixel effects, Warp effects, Moving and linking styles, Sticky styles, Reducing and clearing styles, Making and saving styles, Over-riding character color, Filter introduction, Creating trim marks, Pen and ink, More lignifications, The Blend Tool, Blending introduction, Blending multiple objects, Customizing the Keyboard, Creating your own shortcuts

CONTENTS

Short Questions

Q1. What is CMYK Image?
A. CMYK Image is used for printing. CMYK mode is used for preparing an image to print using process colors.

Q2. Define blending modes.
A. Blending modes are used to determine how two layers are mixed into each other. In Photoshop we can select from 17 different blending options. Blending modes produce interesting effects.

Q3. What is Pixel?
A. Pixel can be defined as the smallest part of an Image.
A. Pixel is known as the building block of an Image.

Q4. Name any two color modes in Photoshop
A. CMYK, RGB, Lab, Grayscale

Q5. What is direct selection tool in Illustrator?
A. Direct selection tool is used to select the vertex in a shape directly.

Q6. What is blend tool in Illustrator?
A. Blend tool is used to create a tween / transformation between two shapes. With the help of blend tool not only shapes but also color forms a gradient. Blend options also gives a choice to choose steps/distance for transformations.

Q7. What is the full form of PNG & JPEG?
A. JPEG and PNG are image file formats. PNG stands for Portable Network Graphics and JPEG stands for Joint Photographic Expert Group.

Q8. What is the full form of TGA & GIF?
A. TGA and TIF are image file formats. TGA stands for Targa and GIF stands for Graphics Interchange Format.

Q9. What is the full form of TIFF & BMP?
A. TIFF and BMP are image file formats. TIFF stands for Tagged Image Format File and BMP stands for Bit Map File.

Q10.	What is the full form of PSD & AI?
A. PSD and AI are software open file formats. PSD stands for Photoshop Document, open file for Photoshop and AI stands for Adobe Illustrator, open file for Adobe Illustrator.

Q11.	What is the full form of SVG & EPS?
A. SVG stands for Saleable Vector Graphics and EPS stands for Encapsulate Post Script.

Q12.	What is the full form of XML & PDF?
A. XML stands for Extensible Markup Language and PDF stands for Portable Document Format.

Q13.	What do CMYK and RGB stand for?
A. CMYK stands for Cyan Magenta Yellow Key (Krypton / blacK / blanK) and RGB stands for Red, Green and Blue.

Q14.	What do CG and CGI stand for?
A. CG stands for Computer Graphics and CGI stands for Computer Generated Imagery.

Q15.	What do BPC and PSB stand for?
A. BPC stands for Bits per Channel and PSB stands for Photoshop Big.

Q16.	Define Vector with respect to graphics?
A. Vector is a saleable file format. Vectors are made of dots with mathematical calculations, which are saleable. Vectors are not made of pixels; hence they are free from pixilation.

Q17.	What is Raster?
A. Raster is made of pixels. Pixel is the smallest unit of an image. On scaling raster we have pixilation problem.

Q18.	Define Graphics?
A. Graphic is visual representation of a design with a minimum of two colors or shades. We have two kinds of graphics namely Vector and Raster.

Q19.   Explain bpc.
A. bpc stands for bits per channel. It represents numbers of bits each channel holds in an image. bpc defines the number of colors and shades that can exist in an image.

Q20.   Why do we use RGB?
A. CMYK is used for digital image work. If we want to use design/graphic only for digital purpose, e.g., Phone, Social Media, Internet, Digital photo frame, Television or any other digital medium we use RGB color mode.

Q21. Define Resolution.
A. Resolution is defined as pixels per inch i.e., number of pixels in one inch of an area. Higher resolution leads to higher number of pixels and better the image quality and vice versa.

Q22.   What is PAR?
A. PAR stands for Pixel Aspect Ratio. PAR defines the shape of the Pixel.

Q23.   Explain brush stroke with respect to Photoshop.
A. Brush Stoke option in Photoshop is used to give variation in brush strokes. It helps in defining various properties of brush like scatter, size, rotation, hue, saturation and texture.

Q24.   Name two masks in Photoshop.
A. Vector Mask, Clipping Mask, Layer Mask

Q25.   What is Quick Mask used for?
A. Quick Mask tool is used for selection process. It helps in selecting complex shapes with the help of a brush by creating a mask like selection over it.

Q26.   Name two selection tools in Photoshop.
A. Marquee Tool, Lasso Tool, Magic Wand and Quick Mask.

Q27.   How many colors can a 1 bit image contain? Name them
A. Two Colors. They are Black & White.

Q28.   How many are there in 1 bpc? Name them
A. Two Colors. They are Black & White.

Q29.   How many colors and shades are there in 8 bit image?
A. 256 Shades.

Q30.   How many colors and shades are there in 16 bit image?
A. 65536 Shades.

Q31.   What is Adobe Photoshop?
A. Adobe Photoshop is an image editing software developed by Adobe. Using Adobe Photoshop image adjustment, modification and editing can be done.

Q32.   How to re-size image in Photoshop?
A. To resize an image in Photoshop you have to go into menu bar, in that "Image Size". This opens the dialog box with options to adjust the image size.

Q33.   What is a Gradient in Adobe Photoshop?
A. Gradient is a smooth blending of shades from light to dark color or from one color to another color. Gradients are used to create great eye-catching graphics. There are five types of gradients in Photoshop namely, Linear, Radial, Diamond, Angular and Reflected.

Q34.   Name the elements of Photoshop's work area?
A. The Photoshop's work area includes Application Bar, Option Bar, Panel Dock and Tools panel.

Q35.   What is resizing images and what are the parameters to change the size of the picture?
A. Resizing of an image is done to suit a particular purpose of the application. The parameters to change the size of image are:
Image Size
Resolution of Image
Pixels in an Image

Q36.   How to organize layers in Photoshop?

A. A picture or image is stored in a layer in Photoshop. To organize layers in Photoshop, place various images, texts in separate layers. Create a folder and rename it. Select the layers you want to keep together and move them in the folder.

Q37.   In Photoshop, what is a smart object?
A. Smart object is a special layer known as Smart Object Layer. It gives freedom to work with multiple copies of the object with the benefit of updating all the copies by updating just one copy. There is no loss of pixel in resizing. It was introduces from   Photoshop CS2 onwards.

Q38.   How to print the grid in Adobe Photoshop?
A. First of all you have to place the non-printing grid in a manner you want the print, and then take a screen shot. Now, you have to open a new file and paste your screen shot image on it. Once done, you can crop the background of the Photoshop window except the image with the grid. The image is ready for print.

Q39.   How to unlock the background in Photoshop?
A. To unlock the background image, double click on the background layer, options will appear, click OK. Background layer is unlocked.

Q40.   What is the difference between PSB (Photoshop Big) and PSD (Photoshop Document)?
A. PSB & PSD are both Photoshop file formats to store digital images. PSD is a default extension for Photoshop files and it can support the file size of 30,000 by 30,000 pixels. While for creating big documents or large image .psb file format is used, and it can save an image size up to 300,000 by 300,000 pixels.

Q41.   What is healing tool?
A. Healing tool is used in Photoshop to hide the unwanted spots on original picture and makes picture look like real without any changes. The tool use complicated algorithm to calculate what would be the color and texture of the area of your picture based on the surrounding pixels.

Q42.   Can graphic tablet be used in Photoshop?

A. Yes, graphic tablet can be used in Photoshop. After installing the graphic tablet drivers, open and configure the hot keys.

Q43.   How to reduce noise in an image?
A. Reduce noise option is helpful to reduce the color and luminance effect in the image. To reduce the noise in an image, you have to go in a menu bar, select a filter menu, in that select Noise menu, in that it will option for reducing noise.

Q44.   How to create an artistic border?
A. To create an artistic border, select an image for which you want to create the border. Add a layer mask to the image. Then select filter > brush strokes > sprayed strokes.

Q45.   What is Gaussian blur?
A. Gaussian blur is used to blur the edges of the image to make it real and adaptive to the surrounding. Gaussian blur if used intelligently it enhances the appearance of the image.

Q46.   What is swatches palette?
A. Swatch Palette is used to get specific colors without remembering their numeric values. Swatch Palette also stores colors extracted from an image.

Q47.   What is Lasso tool? Name the available lasso tools.
A. Lasso tool is used to select precise area of an image. It is used to trace the selection outlines to select the area. Available lasso tools are
Simple Lasso Tool   -   Free Hand Selection
Polygonal Lasso Tool   -   Point Based selection
Magnetic Lasso Tool   -   Calculations based on setting for selection.

Q48.   How Magnetic Lasso Tool works?
A. Magnetic lasso tool uses mathematical calculations, depending on the selected settings, to identify the color difference at the edges for selection.

Q49.   How to create a transparent background in Photoshop?

A. To create transparent image, first select the image, then Inverse (Ctrl + I) the selection. Now your background is selected. Delete the background. Save the image in .psd or .png or any other transparency supported image format. Image with transparent background is ready.

Q50.   What is Clone tool?
A. Clone tool uses clone brush to repair the problem area. Clone brush samples area of an image and copies the same on the problem area. Alt + Click sample the area.

Q51.   How to fix the blurry images in Photoshop?
A. To fix the blurry images in Photoshop you can use sharpening tools. Sharpening the image will lose the pixels, make sure you are finished with everything else and saved the changes before you start sharpening the image.

Q52.   How to combine images?
A. Auto-blend layers option is used to combine images. Auto-blend layers uses layer masks as needed to mask-out overexposed and underexposed areas.

Q53.   What is a Bezier curve?
A. Bezier curve is a mathematically defined curve. Bezier curve is a curve with Bezier handles. Bezier handles are used to define the smoothness of the curve.

Q54.   How Red Eye tool works?
A. Red eye tool is used to remove the red eye problem from the image. When we click on the red eye using red eye tool Photoshop will automatically identity that area and will replace it by dark-gray pixels.

Q55.   Define Path?
A. A path can be defined as a collection of possibly disconnected, lines and areas describing the image. In simple words, it is a collection of curves and line segments arranged on the page.

Q56.   Explain how to create a Diptych?
A. To create a Diptych

Go to Print > layout style > Custom Package > Rulers, Grids and Guides (check the required options) then adjust settings according to desired output. Then drop the image on film strip and arrange as per requirement. Then to export the file, choose Print to File.

Q57.   What color is considered to be blown out?
A. Any color whose value exceeds 240 is considered as blown out color.

Q58.   Write the important applications of computer graphic?
A. Following are the applications of computer graphic
1. Computer graphics is used to produce illustrations.
2. Computer graphic are used for commercial applications and product promotions.
3. Computer graphics are used in combination with 3D applications for creating textures, backgrounds, motion graphics, music videos and television shows.

Q59.   How to change canvas size?
A. To change canvas size, choose Image > Canvas Size. Make necessary changes in the dialogue box and click ok.

Q60.   List any four hardware devices used for computer graphic
A. The hardware devices used for the computer graphics are Keyboard, Mouse, Data tablet, Scanner, Light pen, Touch screen, Joystick.
    Raster Devices- CRT, LCD, LED, Plasma screens, Printers
    Vector Devices- Plotters, Oscilloscopes

Q61.   What are the advantages of electrostatic plotters?
A. Advantages of electrostatic plotters are
1. They are faster than pen plotters and very high quality printers.
2. Recent electrostatic plotters include a scan conversion capability.
3. Color electrostatic plotters are available. They make multiple passes over the paper to plot color picture.

Q62.   What is scan code?

A. When a key is pressed on the keyboard, the keyboard controller places a code corresponding to the key pressed in part of the memory called as the keyboard buffer. This code is called as scan code.

Q63.   How and where in Photoshop is Color information stored?
A. In Photoshop, Color information is stored with the help of pixels on Layers. One pixel can hold only one color value or information.

Q64.   Explain Dual Brush.
A. Dual brush uses attributes to create multiple brush marks in the brush stroke. Using dual brush attributes, two brushes can be selected and used to create brush stroke at the same time.

Q65.   What is the shortcut key used to create a new canvas in Photoshop?
A. Ctrl + N is the shortcut key used to create new canvas in Photoshop.

Q66.   Which selection tool does not have feather option?
A. Magic wand tool does not have feather option.

Q67.   What tool is used for cropping multiple images to the same dimensions?
A. Crop tool is the best option for cropping multiple images in the same dimensions. Crop tool has option for fixed dimension, on selecting the option, dimensions get fixed and all images get cropped in the same dimensions.

Q68.   Explain Quick mask mode.
A. Quick mask mode (Q) is a selection mode. Quick mask is used for complex selection. Quick mask uses black and white color with brush tool. Paint with Black to add mask, mask addition shows in red color and paint with White to remove mask.

Q69.   Explain Vector Mask.
A. Vector masks uses vector shapes to mask or hide the unwanted area of an image. Vector mask can be altered with the pen tool.

Q70.   Explain Layer Mask.

A. Layer mask can be used to hide or mask unwanted area of an image. Layer mask uses brush tool to hide/unhide the area. Black color hides the area and White color is used unhide the area.

Q71.   Short cut key to Invert colors in Photoshop?
A. Ctrl + I is used to invert color in Photoshop.

Q72.   Short cut key to invert selection in Photoshop?
A. Ctrl + Shift + I is used to invert selection in Photoshop.

Q73.   Canvas size in Photoshop is Width: 2 inch, Height: 1 inch, Resolution: 15. Calculate the total numbers of pixels in whole image.
A. Image will have 450 pixels.
Solution,   Given,
    Width = 2 Inch
    Height = 1 Inch
    Resolution = 15
By definition Resolution is Pixels per Inch
Therefore,
    Number of Pixels in Width   =   2 * 15 =   30
Pixels
    Number of Pixels in Height   =   1 * 15 =   15
Pixels
    Total Number of Pixels in Image   = No. of Pixels in Width *
No. of Pixels in Height

                                       =   30 * 15
                                       =   450 Pixels

Q.74   Name any three file formats that support image transparency.
A. File formats that support image transparency are PNG, TGA, and TIFF.

Q75.   In Photoshop, How many points can be added in a Curve?
A. Curve (Ctrl + M) can have a maximum of 16 points in Photoshop.

Q76.   What is shortcut of filling background in a canvas or selected area?

A. Shortcut to fill background color is Ctrl + Backspace, Ctrl + Delete can also be used to fill background color.

Q77.   What is shortcut of filling foreground in a canvas or selected area?
A. Shortcut to fill foreground color is Alt + Backspace, Alt + Delete can also be used to fill foreground color.

Q78.   How many types of color wheel are there? Name them.
A. There are two types of color wheels, namely Additive color wheel and Subtractive color wheel.

Q79.   How many channels can a JPEG image format contain?
A. JPEG can contain three channels. They are Red, Green and Blue. JPEG file format does not support transparency (Alpha) channel.

Q80.   How many channels can a PNG image format contain?
A. PNG can contain four channels. They are Red, Green, Blue and Alpha. PNG file format supports transparency (Alpha) channel.

Q81.   In Photoshop, how to create Yellow color?
A. In Photoshop, Yellow color can be created by mixing Red and Green colors in equal proportions.

Q82.   In Photoshop, how to create Cyan color?
A. In Photoshop, Cyan color can be created by mixing Blue and Green colors in equal proportions.

Q83.   In Photoshop, how to create Magenta color?
A. In Photoshop, Magenta color can be created by mixing Red and Blue colors in equal proportions.

Q84.   What colors can Alpha channel contain?
A. Alpha channel can contain Black, White and Grey Colors. Black represents transparency, White represents Opaque and Grey represents semi-transparent.

Q85.   In Photoshop, What is the shortcut of Lasso tool?
A. L is the shortcut for lasso tool.

Q86.	In Photoshop, What is the shortcut of Polygon Lasso tool?
A. L is the shortcut for polygon lasso tool.

Q87.	In Photoshop, What is the shortcut of Magnetic Lasso tool?
A. L is the shortcut for magnetic lasso tool.

Q88.	In Photoshop, What is the shortcut of Spot healing brush tool?
A. J is the shortcut for spot healing brush tool.

Q89.	In Photoshop, What is the shortcut of Patch tool?
A. J is the shortcut for Patch tool.

Q90.	In Photoshop, What is the shortcut of Red eye tool?
A. J is the shortcut for red eye tool.

Q91.	In Photoshop, What is the shortcut of Clone stamp tool?
A. S is the shortcut for clone stamp tool.

Q92.	In Photoshop, What is the shortcut of Burn tool?
A. O is the shortcut for burn tool.

Q93.	In Photoshop, What is the shortcut of Rectangle Marquee tool?
A. M is the shortcut for Rectangle marquee tool.

Q94.	In Photoshop, What is the shortcut of Magic Wand tool?
A. W is the shortcut for Magic Wand tool.

Q95.	In Photoshop, What is the shortcut of Background Eraser tool?
A. E is the shortcut for Background Eraser tool.

Q96.	In Photoshop, What is the shortcut of Magic Eraser tool?
A. E is the shortcut for Magic Eraser tool.

Q97.	In Photoshop, What is the shortcut of Art History Brush tool?

A. Y is the shortcut for Art History Brush tool.

Q98.   In Photoshop, What is the shortcut of Eye Dropper tool?
A. I is the shortcut for Eye Dropper tool.

Q99.   In Photoshop, What is the shortcut of Ruler tool?
A. I is the shortcut for Ruler tool.

Q100.   In Photoshop, What is the shortcut of Crop tool?
A. C is the shortcut for Crop tool.

Q101.   In Photoshop, What is the shortcut of Slice tool?
A. C is the shortcut for Slice tool.

Q102.   In Photoshop, What is the shortcut of Gradient tool?
A. G is the shortcut for Gradient tool.

Q103.   In Photoshop, What is the shortcut of Paint Bucket tool?
A. G is the shortcut for Paint Bucket tool.

Q104.   In Photoshop, What is the shortcut of Pen tool?
A. P is the shortcut for Pen tool.

Q105.   In Photoshop, What is the shortcut of Horizontal Type tool?
A. T is the shortcut for Horizontal Type tool.

Q106.   In Photoshop, What is the shortcut of Vertical Type tool?
A. T is the shortcut for Vertical Type tool.

Q107.   In Photoshop, What is the shortcut of Path Selection tool?
A. A is the shortcut for Path Selection tool.

Q108.   In Photoshop, What is the shortcut of Direct Selection tool?
A. A is the shortcut for Direct Selection tool.

Q109.   In Photoshop, What is the shortcut of Rectangle tool?
A. U is the shortcut for Rectangle tool.

Q110.   In Photoshop, What is the shortcut of Pencil tool?

A. B is the shortcut for Pencil tool.

Q111.	In Photoshop, What is the shortcut of Brush tool?
A. B is the shortcut for Brush tool.

Q112.	In Photoshop, What is the shortcut of Zoom tool?
A. Z is the shortcut for Zoom tool.

Q113.	In Photoshop, What is the shortcut of Hand tool?
A. H is the shortcut for Hand tool.

Q114.	In Photoshop, What is the shortcut of Rotate View tool?
A. R is the shortcut for Rotate View tool.

Q115.	In Photoshop, What is the shortcut to change Image size?
A. Alt + Ctrl + I is the shortcut used to change Image size

Q116.	In Photoshop, What is the shortcut to change Canvas size?
A. Alt + Ctrl + C is the shortcut used to change Canvas size

Q117.	In Photoshop, What is the shortcut to access Levels?
A. Ctrl + L is the shortcut used to access Levels.

Q118.	In Photoshop, What is the shortcut to access Curves?
A. Ctrl + M is the shortcut used to access Curves.

Q119.	In Photoshop, What is the shortcut to access Hue & Saturation?
A. Ctrl + U is the shortcut used to access Hue & Saturation.

Q120.	In Photoshop, What is the shortcut to Desaturate an image?
A. Ctrl + Shift + U is the shortcut used to access Desaturate an image.

Q121.	In Photoshop, What is the shortcut to access Color Balance?
A. Ctrl + B is the shortcut used to access Color Balance.

Q122.	In Photoshop, What is the shortcut to invert colors?
A. Ctrl + I is the shortcut used to Invert colors.

Q123.	In Photoshop, What is the shortcut to create new layer?
A. Ctrl + N is the shortcut used to create new layer.

Q124.	In Photoshop, What is the shortcut for Layer via Copy?
A. Ctrl + J is the shortcut used for Layer via Copy.

Q125.	In Photoshop, What is the shortcut to access Vanishing Point?
A. Alt + Ctrl + V is the shortcut used to access Vanishing Point.

Q126.	In Photoshop, What is the shortcut to access Liquify?
A. Shift + Ctrl + X is the shortcut used to access Liquify.

Q127.	In Photoshop, What is the shortcut to access Lens Correction?
A. Shift + Ctrl + R is the shortcut used to access Lens Correction.

Q128.	In Photoshop, What is the shortcut for Adaptive Wide Angle?
A. Shift + Ctrl + A is the shortcut for Adaptive Wide Angle.

Q129.	In Photoshop, What is the shortcut to Find Layer?
A. Alt + Ctrl + Shift + F is the shortcut to Find Layer.

Q130.	In Photoshop, What is the shortcut to Merge Layers?
A. Ctrl + E is the shortcut to Merge Layers.

Q131.	In Photoshop, What is the shortcut to Merge Visible Layers?
A. Shift + Ctrl + E is the shortcut to Merge Visible Layers.

Q132.	In Photoshop, What is the shortcut to Repeat Last Filter?
A. Ctrl + F is the shortcut to Repeat Last Filter.

Q133.	In Photoshop, What is the shortcut for Proof Colors?
A. Ctrl + Y is the shortcut for Proof Colors.

Q134.	In Photoshop, What is the shortcut for Gamut Warning?

A. Shift + Ctrl + Y is the shortcut for Gamut Warning.

Q135.   In Photoshop, What is the shortcut to show Ruler?
A. Ctrl + R is the shortcut to show Ruler.

Q136.   In Photoshop, What is the shortcut to show Brush Pallet?
A. F5 is the shortcut to show Brush Pallet.

Q137.   In Photoshop, What is the shortcut to show Brush Pallet?
A. F5 is the shortcut to show Brush Pallet.

Q138.   In Photoshop, What is the shortcut to show Layer Pallet?
A. F7 is the shortcut to show Layer Pallet.

Q139.   In Photoshop, What is the shortcut to show Color Pallet?
A. F6 is the shortcut to show Color Pallet.

Q140.   In Photoshop, What is the shortcut to show Actions Pallet?
A. Alt + F9 is the shortcut to show Actions Pallet.

Q141.   Explain use of Dodge and Burn tools.
A. Dodge tool is used to lighten the color and create a lighter shade.
   Burn tool is used to darken the color and create darker shade.

Q142.   What is the use of 'History Brush Tool'?
A. 'History Brush Tool' is used to draw/create the image from history point set by user/default.

Q143.   What is the use of 'Zoom Tool'?
A. 'Zoom Tool' is used to zoom/focus/concentrate on a specified area. With the help of 'Zoom Tool' we can zoom in or zoom out of the image.

Q144.   Which color mode is used for printing?
A. CMYK is used for color printing.

Q145.   What is the use of filters, in Photoshop?

A. In Photoshop, filters are used to clean, retouch and apply special art effects. Filters are helpful in creating unique transformations, appearance of sketch or painting on the image.

Q146.   What is 'Eye Dropper' used for?
A. Eye Dropper is used to sample a color from image for further usage later. Eye Dropper samples the color information.

Q147.   What is 'Direct' selection tool in Illustrator?
A. Direct selection tool in used to select the anchor point of the shape and edit it, without selection the group.

Q148.   What is outline stroke in Illustrator?
A. Outline stroke in Illustrator is used to give a stroke to the created path. To give stroke path create a shape using pen or pencil tool, then select the shape and go to Object > Path > Outline Stroke.

Q149.   What is Document setup in Illustrator?
A. Document setup in Illustrator is used to create a new document. To create a new document go to File > New and create the desired document size. New document can also be created using template, go to File > New from Template and choose desired template.

Q150.   How to import an image in Illustrator?
A. An image can be imported in Illustrator in multiple ways
➢ Choose the Image in explorer
➢ Click and drag the image in Illustrator
Or
➢ Go to File Menu
➢ Click on Place Image
➢ Select the Image and click Ok

Long Questions

Q1.Explain RGB and CMYK color modes.
A. RGB stands for Red, Green and Blue. RGB color mode is used for digital image work. RGB are the primary colors for additive color theory. RGB can have digitally pure colors and brighter shades compared to CMYK.

CMYK stands for Cyan, Magenta, Yellow and Key. CMYK color mode is used for printing and publishing. CMY are the secondary colors for digital color theory. CMYK has purest form of printable colors. CMYK dyes are used for screen and offset printing.

Q2.Write short notes on Computer Graphics.
A. Computer Graphics is the term used to define almost everything on computer that is not text or sound. CG is the art of drawing pictures, graphics, lines, charts, illustrations, etc. using computers. Computer Graphics can also be defined as the manipulation and representation of image data by computer with the help from specialized software and hardware. Computer graphics help us in getting the real display experiences. Computer Graphics require use of specific software like Photoshop, Illustrator, CorelDraw, etc.

Q3.How to create a pattern?
A. To create a pattern in Photoshop, First create a desired design or import the graphic, which has to be converted into a pattern. Then using rectangle Marquee tool creates a selection of the desired area. Now go to Edit > Define Pattern. Enter desired name for the pattern in the dialogue box. Pattern is ready
To create a pattern in Illustrator, select the artwork to create pattern, and then choose Object > Pattern > Make. Make necessary changes to the options in the dialog box and click ok. Pattern is ready.

Q4. Explain what is PostScript and showpage command?
A. PostScript is a page description language developed by Adobe Systems. It is a language for printing documents on laser printer, but it can also be used to produce images on other types of devices. Showpage command transfers the contents of the current page to the current output device. The main function of showpage is

• It executes the endpage procedure in the page device dictionary
• Executes the function equivalent of an initgraphics operation, reinitializing the graphics state for the next page
• In page device dictionary, it executes the beginpage
• If the Boolean result returned by the EndPage process is true, transmits the contents of the page to the current output device and performs the equivalent of an erasepage operation, clearing the contents in preparation for the next page.

Q5. What are raster and vector graphics? Explain
A. Raster and Vector graphics can be explained as

RASTER- Raster is an image made up of Pixels. In computer graphics image, or BITMAP, is a dot matrix data structure representing a generally rectangular grid of pixels or points of color, viewable via a monitor, paper, or other display medium. Raster image are stored in image files with varying formats. Raster image pixilates on zooming.

VECTOR- Vector graphics is the use of geometrical primitives such as points, lines, curves, and shapes or polygon, which are all based on mathematical expressions, to represent image in computer graphics. "Vector", in this context, implies more than a straight line. Vectors can be scaled without the loss of quality.

Q6. Differentiate between vector and raster graphics?
A.

S.No.	Raster Graphics	Vector Graphics
1	Raster or Bitmap images are resolution dependent because of this it's not possible to increase or decrease their size without sacrificing on image quality.	Vector based image are not dependent on resolution. The size of vector image can be increased or decreased without affecting image quality.
2	Raster or bitmap images are always rectangular in shape	Vector image, however, can have any shape.
3	Raster or bitmap images haves realistic colors and shades.	Vector images are made up of solid color areas and mathematical gradients, so they can't be used to show continuous tones of colors in a

		natural photograph.

Q7. Define scaling with respect to computer graphics.

A. Image scaling is the process of resizing a digital image. Scaling is a non-trivial process that involves a trade-off between efficiency, smoothness and sharpness. With bitmap graphics, as the size of an image is reduced or enlarged, the pixels which comprise the image become increasingly visible, making the image appear "soft" if pixels are averaged, or jagged if not.

Q8. Define Random and Raster scan displays?

A. Random scan is a method in which display is made by electronic beam, which is directed only to the points or parts of the screen where picture is to be drawn.

The Raster scan system is a scanning technique in which there is electron sweep from top to bottom and from left to right. The intensity is turned on or off to light and unlight/darken the pixel.

Q9. Explain difference between Layer via Copy and Duplicate layer.

A. In Photoshop, Layer via Copy and Duplicate Layer are two options to copy a layer. We can copy any layer and create its duplicate with the help of any of these two options. However, there is a lot difference between the ways these two options work. If a layer has to be copied on to a new canvas or file then duplicate layer is used. If the layer is to be duplicated on the same canvas or file then any of the option between layer via copy and duplicate can be used.

Q10.   Write short notes on HSV color space.

A. HSV stands for hue, saturation and value. It is also known as HSB (B for brightness). Developed in the 1970s, HSV is used in image editing software, in color pickers and less commonly in image analysis and computer vision.

Hue: Hue is one of the main properties of a color, defined technically, as "the degree to which a stimulus can be described as similar to or different from stimuli that are described as Red, green, blue, and yellow".

Saturation: The saturation of a color is determined by a combination of light intensity and how much it is distributed across the spectrum of different wavelengths. The purest (most saturated) color is achieved by using just one wavelength at a high intensity, such as in laser light.

<u>Value:</u> The brightness of the color ranges from 0 to 100% is referred as value of color.

Q11.   Explain 'Adjustment Layer' option.

A. An adjustment layer is used to apply color and tonal adjustments to an image without changing pixel values. It is a non destructive way of image editing. For example, instead of applying Levels or Curves adjustment directly to image, you can create a Levels or Curves adjustment layer. The color and tonal adjustments are stored in the adjustment layer and apply to all the layers below it; multiple layers can be corrected by making a single adjustment, rather than adjusting each layer separately. Adjustments and changes can be discarded and original image can be restored at any time.

Adjustment layer can also be used for selective editing. Paint on the adjustment layer's image mask to apply an adjustment to part of an image, which can be edited later to control the parts of an image. Adjustment layers have characteristics like opacity and blending mode. Adjustment layers can also be turned on and off to view their effect.

Q12.   Explain 'Pen Tool'.

A. Photoshop provides multiple Pen tools. They are Pen Tool, Freeform Pen Tool and Magnetic Pen.

<u>Pen Tool:</u> Pen tool is used to draw with greatest precision. Pen tool places anchor points, to define the initial coordinates of a path segment. Pen tool can also be used to Add Anchor Point and Delete Anchor point tools as well. The keyboard shortcut for the Pen Tool is 'P'.

<u>Freeform Pen Tool:</u> The Freeform Pen Tool works as if drawing with a pencil or pen on a paper. Anchor points are added automatically while drawing. Anchor points can be adjusted once the path is complete.

<u>Magnetic Pen:</u> Magnetic Pen lets you draw a path that snaps to the edges of defined areas in your image. Anchor points are added

automatically while drawing. Anchor points can be adjusted once the path is complete.

Q13.	Explain 'Path'.

A. Paths are common to many types of computer graphics programs; they are used extensively in digital illustration, page layout, 3D modeling and all types of animation related software. Photoshop and Illustrator are software that commonly uses paths. Paths are mathematically defined. The shape of a Path is based on mathematical concept called vectors. To understand simply, a vector is a geometric object usually represented by a line that has both a direction and defined length. Paths are resolution- independent and flexible.

Q14.	Explain 'Path Selection Tool'.

A. When creating vector objects, both the Pen tool and Path Selection tool utilize some important Path modification Features, found on the Options bar when either tool is selected.

Auto Add/Delete: When you move your cursor over an existing anchor point, the cursor changes into the Delete Anchor Point tool (click on the point, and it's deleted). This happens because there is a checkbox called Auto Add/Delete on the Pen tool options bar which is turned on by default.

Add to path area (+): To create and name a path, make sure no work path is selected. Choose New Path from the Paths panel menu, or Alt-click (Windows) or Option-click (Mac OS) the New Path button at the bottom of the panel. Enter a name for the path in the New Path dialog box, and click OK.

Subtract from path area (-): This property is usually applied to path components the shape and area for which need to be removed from a pre-existing Path component.

Intersect Path areas: This property is usually applied to path components that are intended to redefine the shape of a path by eliminating from the new path area all other areas that do not overlap one another.

<u>Exclude Overlapping Path Area</u>: This property is usually applied to path components that are intended to redefine the shape of a path by eliminating from the new path area all other areas that do overlap. In essence this is the opposite of creating a new Path via Intersect Path Areas.

Q15.   What is the use of 'Vanishing Point'? Explain in brief.
A. Vanishing Point simplifies perspective correction and editing in images that contain perspective planes. In Vanishing Point, you specify the planes in an image, and then apply edits such as painting, cloning, copying or pasting, and transforming. All your edits honor the perspective of the plane you're working in. When you retouch, add, or remove content in an image, the results are more realistic because the edits are properly oriented and scaled to the perspective planes. After you finish working in Vanishing Point, you can continue editing the image in Photoshop. To preserve the perspective plane information in an image, save your document. To access Vanishing Point dialog box go to Filter > Vanishing Point. Vanishing point dialogue box contains tools for defining the perspective planes, tools for editing the image, a measure tool, and an image preview.

Q16.   Explain 'Clone Stamp Tool'.
A. Clone Stamp Tool paints with sampled pixels of an image. Following steps are to use Clone Stamp Tool
- Open an image.
- From the Toolbox, select Clone Stamp Tool.
- In Options bar, set tools tip size and hardness.
- Point the cursor at the image area you want to paint with, hold down [Alt] key, then Mouse - click. You have just selected the source point for cloning.
- Paint with the copied pixels.
- The "Aligned" Option, forces the source point to follow your mouse, even after you complete a stroke. In other words, every new stroke continues the image started by the first stroke.
- Deselecting the "Aligned" option starts the sample point back to its original location every time you release the mouse button. That is, every new stroke re-starts cloning your image from the source point.

Q17.   What is Layer Style? Explain any two layer styles.

A. Layer styles are special effects that can be quickly and easily applied to individual layers in Photoshop to drastically change the appearance of something in very little time. They can be preset, customized, or even saved and used for later. Layer style has many options. To apply Layer Style choose Layer>Layer Style>Gradient Overlay/ Stroke (Layer Style Option).

Q18.   What is 'Kerning'? Explain in brief with example.

A. Kerning is the process of adjusting space between letters or characters, to achieve a visually pleasing result. Kerning adjusts space between individual letters, while tracking adjusts space uniformly over a range of characters. Letter Spacing values can range from –100% to 500%; at 0%, no space is added between letters; at 100%, an entire space width is added between letters.

Example: HELLO WORLD   –   Kerning   – Normal

         HELLO WORLD –   Kerning   – Expanded

         HELLO WORLD   –   Kerning   – Condensed

Q19.   What are blending modes?

A. Blend modes in digital image editing are used to determine how two layers are blended or mixed into each other. Photoshop has 17 different blending options to affect how the Image data in a Layer mixes or blends with other Layers. Blending Modes require at least two layers to produce interesting results. Blend Modes produces interesting effects depending on their group classification. Blending modes can be classified / grouped as

➢ Normal
   - Normal
   - Dissolve
➢ Darken
   - Darken
   - Multiply
   - Color Burn
   - Linear Burn
   - Barker Color

- ➢ Lighten
  - ▪ Lighten
  - ▪ Screen
  - ▪ Dodge
  - ▪ Linear Dodge (Add)
  - ▪ Lighter Color
- ➢ Contrast
  - ▪ Overlay
  - ▪ Soft Light
  - ▪ Hard Light
  - ▪ Vivid Light
  - ▪ Linear Light
  - ▪ Pin Light
  - ▪ Hard Mix
- ➢ Inversion
  - ▪ Difference
  - ▪ Exclusion
- ➢ Cancelation
  - ▪ Subtract
  - ▪ Divide
- ➢ Component
  - ▪ Hue
  - ▪ Saturation
  - ▪ Color
  - ▪ Luminosity

Q20.   Why Photoshop is mostly used in Animation Industry?

A. Photoshop is a raster based image editing software. It is widely used for editing images, creating Matte Paintings, Digital Paintings, illustrations, textures, storyboards, concept art, character sheet, etc. Photoshop has following applications in Animation Industry.

<u>Matte Painting:</u> Matte Painting is widely used in animation industry. Matte Painting is an imaginary background used in films, T.V series, commercials etc. Matte Painting is created with the help of various images and use of imagination.

<u>Digital Painting:</u> Digital Painting is an important part of animation industry. Digital Painting is a visual representation of artist's creativity

and imagination to be used in films, T.V series, commercials etc. Digital Painting is a painting created digitally, i.e., with the help of computer based software.

<u>Textures:</u> Textures are used in animation industry for the purpose of texturing. Texturing is the process of defining the look and feel of an object in 3D software. Textures are created using Photoshop.

Q21.   Write process of converting Black & White to Color image?
A. Photoshop is used to convert image from Black and White to Color
➢ Open the image in Photoshop.
➢ Go to Image>Adjustments>Black & White.
➢ Adjust the value of each color till desired colors are attained.
➢ Make other necessary adjustments like exposure, contrast, etc.
➢ Save the result.

Q22.   Explain in brief 'filters'.
A. A filter is a particular effect that can be applied to an image or part of an image. Filters can be simple effects used to mimic photographic filters or they can be complex programs used to create painterly effects. Filters can be used to clean up or retouch photos, apply special art effects to give appearance of a sketch or impressionistic painting. Filters are used to create unique transformations using distortions and lighting effects. The filters appear in the Filter menu. Smart Filters, applied to Smart Objects, let you use filters non-destructively. Smart Filters are stored as layer effects in the Layers panel and can be readjusted at any time, working from the original image data contained in the Smart Object.

Q23.   What is Batch Processing? Explain.
A. The Batch command runs an action on a folder of files. If you have a digital camera or a scanner with a document feeder, you can also import and process multiple images with a single action. Steps to Batch-process files
➢ Choose File > Automate > Batch (Photoshop)
➢ Specify the action to process files from the Set and Action pop-up menus.

- ➢ Choose the files to process from the Source pop-up menu:
  - Folder: Processes files in a folder you specify. Click Choose to locate and select the folder.
  - Import: Processes images from a digital camera, scanner, or a PDF document.
  - Opened Files: Processes all open files.
- ➢ Set processing, saving, and file naming options.

Q24.   Explain how to customize shortcut in Photoshop.

A. Photoshop allows user to customize shortcuts according to preferences. To customize shortcuts in Photoshop follow the steps

- ➢ Go to any one of the following
  - Edit > Keyboard Shortcuts.
  - Window > Workspace > Keyboard Shortcuts & Menus and click the Keyboard Shortcuts tab.
- ➢ Select set of shortcuts from the Set menu.
- ➢ Select shortcut type from the Shortcuts For menu:
  - Application Menus: Lets you customize keyboard shortcuts for items in the menu bar.
  - Panel Menus: Lets you customize keyboard shortcuts for items in panel menus.
  - Tools: Lets you customize keyboard shortcuts for tools in the toolbox.
- ➢ Select the shortcut to modify.
- ➢ Type a new shortcut.
- ➢ If the shortcut is already assigned to another command or tool, an alert appears. Click Accept to assign the shortcut.
- ➢ After finishing changes to shortcuts, do one of the following:
  - Save Set: Changes to a custom set are saved.
  - Save Set As: New keyboard shortcut set will be saved.
  - Undo: To discard the last saved change.
  - Use Default: To set a new shortcut to the default.
  - Cancel: To discard all changes and exit.

Q25.   Explain 'save to web option'.

A. 'Save for Web' option is used to optimize image for web. Save for Web does following.

- ➢ It optimizes the file dimensions allowing it to fit into web pages.
- ➢ It optimizes the file size allowing it to download/load faster.

➤ It saves in the RGB format as opposed to the CMYK (print) format.

'Save for Web' works great for images to be uploaded for web. Optimized file formats are .JPEG, .PNG and .GIF.

Q26.   Explain 'Animation' option in Photoshop.

A. 'Animation' option is used to create animation clips and videos in Photoshop. This option is helpful in creating .GIF and videos for web. Photoshop supports frame-based animation and key based animation. To create animation in Photoshop, use the following general workflow.

➤ Open a new document.
➤ Open the Timeline, and Layers panels.
➤ Change Timeline panel to frame animation mode.
➤ Click the down pointing arrow to choose Create Frame Animation and then click the button next to the arrow.
➤ Add a layer.
➤ Add content to your animation.
➤ Add a frame to the Timeline panel.
➤ Select a frame.
➤ Edit the layers for the selected frame.
  ▪ Turn visibility on and off for different layers.
  ▪ Change the position of objects or layers to make layer content move.
  ▪ Change layer opacity to make content fade in or out.
  ▪ Change the blending mode of layers.
  ▪ Add a style to layers.
➤ Add more frames and edit layers as needed.
➤ Set frame delay and looping options.
➤ Preview the animation.
➤ Save For Web.
➤ Optimize the animation for efficient download.
➤ Save the animation.
  ▪ Save as an animated GIF using the Save for Web command.
  ▪ Save in Photoshop (PSD) format so you can do more work on the animation later.
  ▪ Save as an image sequence, QuickTime movie, or as separate files. See also Export video files or image sequences.

Q27.   Explain lighting effect of filter in Render option.

A. The Lighting Effects filter lets you produce myriad lighting effects on RGB images. You can also use textures from grayscale files (called bump maps) to produce 3D-like effects and save your own styles for use in other images. To apply Lighting Effect, follow the steps

➢ Choose Filter > Render > Lighting Effects.
➢ From the Presets menu at upper left, choose a style.
➢ Select individual lights to adjust.
➢ In Properties panel, adjust the following:
  ▪ Choose a light type (Spot, Infinite, or Point).
  ▪ Adjust color, intensity, and hotspot size.
  ▪ Colorize: Click to tint the overall lighting.
  ▪ Exposure: Controls highlight and shadow detail.
  ▪ Gloss: Determines how much surfaces reflects light.
  ▪ Metallic: Determines which is more reflective: the light or the object.
  ▪ Ambience: Diffuses the light as if it were combined with other light in a room.
  ▪ Texture: Applies a texture channel.

Q28.   Explain Histogram.

A. Histogram displays the tonal values / range of the image. Histogram illustrates how pixels in an image are distributed by graphing the number of pixels at each color intensity level. The histogram shows detail in the shadows, midtones, and highlights. Histogram can help you determine whether an image has enough detail to make a good correction. The histogram also gives a quick picture of the tonal range of the image, or the image key type. A low-key image has detail concentrated in the shadows. A high-key image has detail concentrated in the highlights. An average-key image has detail concentrated in the midtones. An image with full tonal range has some pixels in all areas. Identifying the tonal range helps determine appropriate tonal corrections.

Q29.   Explain Quick Mask Mode.

A. Quick mask mode is a selection mode. Quick Mask mode can be activated with keyboard shortcut Q. It helps in selecting complex shapes with the help of a brush by creating a mask like selection over it. Quick mask uses black and white color with brush tool. Paint with

Black to add mask, mask addition shows in red color and paint with White to remove mask.

Q30.   What is 'Selection Tool'? Explain in brief any four 'Selection Tools'.
A. Selection tool is used to select pixels in an image. Selection tool can be used to make complex selections for image editing, selections can also be made to fill colors and create shapes. Selection tools are

➤ Marquee Selection Tools: The marquee tools select rectangles, ellipses, and 1-pixel rows and columns. Types of Marquee Selection Tools are
  - Rectangular Marquee: Makes a rectangular / square selection.
  - Elliptical Marquee: Makes an elliptical / circle selection.
  - Single Row Marquee: Defines the border as a 1-pixel-wide row.
  - Single Column Marquee: Defines the border as a 1-pixel-wide column.
➤ Lasso Selection Tools: The Lasso tools select freeform, straight-edged and magnetic.
  - Freeform Lasso Tool: The Lasso tool is useful for drawing freeform segments of a selection border.
  - Polygonal Lasso Tool: The Polygonal Lasso tool is useful for drawing straight-edged segments of a selection border.
  - Magnetic Lasso Tool: Magnetic Lasso Tool useful for quickly selecting objects with complex edges set against high-contrast backgrounds. Magnetic Lasso Tool snaps to the edges of defined areas in the image.
➤ Quick Selection Tool: Quick Selection tool, paint a selection using an adjustable round brush tip. Click and drag, and the selection expand outward and automatically finds and follows defined edges in the image.
➤ Magic Wand Tool: Magic Wand selects pixels based on tone and color.

Q31.   What are 'Painting Tools', in Photoshop? Explain in brief.
A. Painting Tools are used to paint pixels in Photoshop. One pixel can hold only one color information. Painting tools help in creating designs, portraits, paintings, image manipulations, shading, etc.

Photoshop has painting tools such as brush tool, pencil tool, paint bucket, stamp tool, art brush tool, fill color and art history brush tool.

Q32.   In Photoshop, Can .JPEG be converted to .PDF? Explain in brief.

A. Yes, In Photoshop .JPEG can be converted to .PDF. Save As command is used to save JPEG format in Photoshop PDF format. Photoshop PDF format supports RGB, indexed-color, CMYK, grayscale, Bitmap-mode, Lab color, and duotone images. Photoshop PDF document can preserve Photoshop data, such as layers, alpha channels, notes, and spot color, you can open the document and edit the images in Photoshop. To convert .JPEG to .PDF in Photoshop following steps need to be followed

➢ Choose File > Save As, and then choose Photoshop PDF from the Format menu.
➢ Click Save.
➢ In the Save Adobe PDF dialog box, choose an Adobe PDF preset.
➢ Choose options from the Standard menu and the Compatibility menu.
➢ Select Compression, specifies the compression and down sampling options for the PDF file. (Optional) To add security (password) to your PDF document, select Security.
➢ Click Save PDF.
➢ Photoshop closes the Save Adobe PDF dialog box and creates the PDF document file.

Q33.   What is text wrap?

A. Text Wrap can be used to wrap text around an object, including type objects, imported images, and objects you draw in Illustrator. If the wrap object is an embedded bitmap image, Illustrator wraps the text around opaque or partially opaque pixels and ignores fully transparent pixels. Wrapping is determined by the stacking order of objects, which you can view in the Layers panel. To wrap text around an object, the wrap object must be in the same layer as the text and located directly above the text in the layer hierarchy. You can drag contents up or down in the Layers panel to change hierarchy. Steps to use text wrap

➢ Text should be in area type (typed in a box).
➢ Text should be in the same layer as the wrap object.

- Text should be located directly under the wrap object in the layer's hierarchy.
- Select the object or objects around which, text has to be wrap.
- Choose Object > Text Wrap > Make.
- Select the wrap object.
- Choose Object > Text Wrap > Text Wrap Options and specify the following options:
    - Offset: Specifies the amount of space between the text and the wrap object. You can enter a positive or negative value.
    - Invert Wrap: Wraps the text around the reverse side of the object.

Q34.   How to apply gradient, in Illustrator?

A. Gradient: This tool (G) is used to adjust the angle of gradients within objects or the start and end points, or apply a gradient to objects. Gradient can be applied to an entire object.

To apply gradient

- Select the object first.
- To apply a fill and not a stroke, click the Fill box in the Tools panel or the Color panel.
- Then Press G or select Gradient to fill gradient.
- Adjust type of gradient from Gradient dialog box.
- Adjust the angle of the gradient.
- Adjust colors and color stops as desired.

Q35.   Explain Pencil Sketch filter.

A. Pencil Sketch filter is used to give pencil drawing like appearance to the image. To apply Sketch filter follow the steps

- Select the layer or area of a layer to apply filter.
- Choose Filter > Filter Gallery>Sketch.
- Select the desired filter.
- Enter values or select options for the filter you selected.
- When satisfied with the results, click OK.

Q36.   In Photoshop, what are 'Actions'? Explain in brief.

A. Actions are recorded tasks, performed frequently to work more efficiently.

Guidelines for recording actions:

- Actions record most but not all commands.

➢ Actions record operations performed with the Marquee, Move, Polygon, Lasso, Magic Wand, Crop, Slice, Magic Eraser, Gradient, Paint Bucket, Type, Shape, Notes, Eyedropper, and Color Sampler tools, History, Swatches, Color, Paths, Channels, Layers, Styles, and Actions panels.

➢ Results depend on file and program setting variables.

➢ Actions cannot record the Play command listed on the Actions panel menu to cause one action to play another.

Q37.   What is the use of 'Sharpen' filter in Photoshop?

A. 'Sharpen' filter is used to sharpen the image. Blur images and photographs sharpen with the use of Sharpen filter. To apply Sharpen filter follow the steps

➢ Select the layer or area of a layer to apply filter.

➢ Choose Filter > Sharpen.

➢ Enter values or select options for the filter you selected.

➢ When satisfied with the results, click OK

Q38.   How to create a pattern in Illustrator?

A. Patters are tile able shapes, which can be repeated infinitely. To create a pattern in Illustrator following are the steps

➢ Create and select art work to create a pattern

➢ Go to Object > Pattern > Make.

To edit an existing pattern,

➢ Double-click the pattern in the pattern swatch

➢ Go to Object > Pattern > Edit Pattern.

➢ Modify the options available in the Pattern Options dialog:

➢ Tile Type:

- Grid: The center of each tile is horizontally and vertically aligned to the center of the adjacent tiles.

- Brick by row: Tiles are rectangular in shape, and arranged in rows. Centers of tiles in rows are horizontally aligned. Centers of tiles in alternate columns are vertically aligned.

- Brick by column: Tiles are rectangular in shape, and arranged in columns. Centers of tiles in columns are vertically aligned. Centers of tiles in alternate columns are horizontally aligned.

- Hex by column: Tiles are hexagonal in shape, and arranged in columns. Centers of tiles in the columns are vertically aligned. Centers of tiles in alternate columns are horizontally aligned.
  - Hex by row: Tiles are hexagonal in shape, and arranged in rows. Centers of tiles in the rows are horizontally aligned. Centers of tiles in alternate rows are vertically aligned.
- Brick Offset:
  - Brick by Row: Determines by how much tile width the centers of tiles in adjacent rows are out of vertical alignment.
  - Brick by Column: Determines by how much tile height the centers of tiles in adjacent columns are out of horizontal alignment.
- Width / Height: Specify the overall height and width of the tile.
- Size Tile to Art: Size of the tile to shrink to the size of the artwork.
- Move Tile with Art: Ensure that moving the artwork causes the tile to move as well.
- H Spacing / V Spacing: Determine space between adjacent tiles.
- Overlap: Determine which tiles appear in front, when adjacent tiles overlap.
- Copies: Number of rows and columns of tiles are visible while modifying the pattern.
- Dim Copies to: Determine the opacity of copies of the artwork tile.
- Show Tile Edge: Displays a box around the tile.
- Show Swatch Bounds: Displays a unit portion of the pattern that is repeated.
- Choose to save or discard changes to the pattern.

Q39.   Explain LAB color mode.

A. Lab Color is a color mode that is not unique to Photoshop. Like other color modes that you may be more familiar with such as RGB and CMYK, Lab Color is a global color model where you can specify any given color by giving numeric values across different channels. A Lab color space is a color-opponent space with dimensions L for lightness and A and B for the color-opponent dimensions, based on nonlinearly compressed coordinates. The LAB color space includes all perceivable colors, which means that its gamut exceeds those of the RGB and CMYK color models. One of the most important attributes of the LAB color is device independence. Lab Color is used for many things outside the realms of photography, digital & print to specify colors because of its accuracy. It is used widely across industries such as the automotive industry, the textile industry and more because it has a wider color gamut than RGB and CMYK. Lab Color is used as the global color mode, which can be matched against all the rest.

Q40.   Explain crop tool in brief.
A. Use the Crop Tool is used to reduce the size of an image, to cut all non-selected content from image. This tool is very useful for tweaking the composition of a photograph as it allows you to remove extraneous material quickly and easily. Cropping is the process of removing portions of a photo to create focus or strengthen the composition. The Crop tool is non-destructive, and you can choose to retain the cropped pixels to optimize the crop boundaries later. The Crop tool also provides intuitive methods to straighten a photo while cropping. The Crop Tool is limited to rectangular shapes.

Q41.   How to use ruler, grid and guides in Illustrator?
A. Ruler helps to accurately place and measure objects in the illustration window or in an artboard. The point where 0 appears on each ruler is called the ruler origin. Illustrator provides separate rulers for documents and artboard. Global rulers appear at the top and left sides of the illustration window. The default ruler origin is located at the top-left corner of the illustration window. The difference between artboard rulers and global rulers is that if you select artboard rulers, the origin point changes based on the active artboard. In addition, you can have different origin points for artboard rulers.
To show or hide rulers, choose View > Rulers > Show Rulers or View> Rulers > Hide Rulers.

Grid appears behind your artwork in the illustration window. Grid helps in placing objects in a design. It does not print.
To show or hide the grid, choose View > Show Grid or View > Hide Grid.

Guides help to align text and graphic objects. Ruler guides and guide objects can be created. Like the grid, guides do not print. Two guide styles are available, dots and lines. Color of guides can be changed. By default, guides are unlocked so that you can move, modify, delete, or revert them, but you can choose to lock them into place.

To show or hide guides, choose View > Guides > Show Guides or View > Guides > Hide Guides.

Q42.   How to convert type into shapes?
A. Type or Text should be converted to shapes before printing. This is important in order to avoid missing fonts and missing font styles. Type can be converted into a set of compound paths or outlines that can be edited and manipulated as any other graphic object. Characters are converted in their current positions, if converted to outlines from type. All graphics formatting such as stroke and fill is retained by them. It is not possible to convert a single letter within a string of type. All the type in a selection needs to be converted. A separate type object containing only that letter needs to be created to convert a single letter into an outline. Select the type object.
Choose Type > Create Outlines.

Q43.   How to apply mask in Illustrator?
A. A clipping mask is defined as an object which clips the artwork to the shape of a mask, in a way that only areas that lie within the shape are visible. Clipping set is defined as a combination of both the clipping mask and the objects that are masked. A clipping set can be prepared from a selection of two or more objects or from all objects in a group or layer. In the layer panel, object level clipping sets are combined as a group. All operations, such as transformation and alignment, which are performed on an object-level clipping set, are based on the clipping mask's boundary and not the unmasked boundary. The clipped content can only be selected by using the Layers panel, the Direct Selection tool or by isolating the clipping set after you have created an object-level clipping mask.

Guidelines to create clipping masks
➤ The objects that are to be masked should be on the same Layer.
➤ Only vector objects can be moved into clipping masks.
➤ Clipping paths can only be vector objects.
➤ The first object in the layer masks everything that is a subset of the layer.
➤ A clipping mask changes to an object with no fill or stroke.

Steps to Create a Clipping Mask

- ➢ Create the object, intended to use as a mask.
- ➢ Move the clipping path above the objects, to mask in the stacking order.
- ➢ Select the objects you want to mask after the clipping path.
- ➢ Select object > Clipping Mask > Make.

Q44.   What is 'Paragraph Formatting'? Explain in brief.

A. 'Paragraph Formatting' is used for formatting a paragraph in a neat and presentable manner. Paragraph formatting is an important part of text editing and presenting. It is widely used in Print Media and Designing industry.

To change the formatting of columns and paragraphs, use the Paragraph panel. Paragraph Panel can be accessed from Window > Type > Paragraph. Options in the Control panel can be to format paragraphs, when type is selected or when the Type tool is active.

Q45.   In Photoshop, what is 'Eraser'? Explain different types of erasers.

A. Eraser is used to remove any image, shape or object. In Photoshop there are three types of Erasers. They are Eraser Tool, Background Eraser Tool and Magic Eraser Tool.

Eraser Tool: Eraser tool changes pixels to either the background color or to transparent. If you're working on a background or in a layer with transparency locked, the pixels change to the background color; otherwise, the pixels are erased to transparency.

Background Eraser tool: Background Eraser tool erases pixels on a layer to transparency as you drag. Background can be erased while maintaining the edges of an object in the foreground, specifying different sampling and tolerance options, can control the range of the transparency and the sharpness of the boundaries.

Magic Eraser tool: Magic Eraser tool erases pixels on a layer to transparency as you click on the color. Single color background can be erased while maintaining the edges of an object in the foreground.

Q46.   In Photoshop, explain 'Non Destructive' editing.

A. An adjustment layer is used to apply color and tonal adjustments to an image without changing pixel values. It is a non destructive way of image editing. For example, instead of applying Levels or Curves adjustment directly to image, you can create a Levels or Curves adjustment layer. The color and tonal adjustments are stored in the adjustment layer and apply to all the layers below it; multiple layers can be corrected by making a single adjustment, rather than adjusting each layer separately. Adjustments and changes can be discarded and original image can be restored at any time.

Adjustment layer can also be used for selective editing. Paint on the adjustment layer's image mask to apply an adjustment to part of an image, which can be edited later to control the parts of an image. Adjustment layers have characteristics like opacity and blending mode. Adjustment layers can also be turned on and off to view their effect.

Q47.   Differentiate between Eraser, Path Eraser and Scissor tool in Illustrator?
A.

Eraser	Path Eraser	Scissor
Eraser is used to erase the art work.	Path Eraser is used to erase a part of the path.	Scissor is used to split the path.
Art work is removed after erasing.	Part of the path is removed and path is split into two parts.	Path is broken into two parts after use of scissor.

Q48.   What are 'Vector Shapes' in Photoshop? Explain in detail.
A. Shapes made of vectors / paths are known as 'Vector Shapes'. Vectors or paths are created using pen tool. Photoshop provides multiple pen tools, namely Pen tool, Freeform Pen Tool and Magnetic Pen Tool. Pen tool is used to draw with greatest precision. The keyboard shortcut for the Pen Tool is 'P'· Paths are mathematically defined. The shape of a Path is based on mathematical concept called vectors. To understand simply, a vector is a geometric object usually represented by a line that has both a direction and defined length. Paths are resolution- independent and flexible.

Q49.   What is 'Channel Calculations'? Explain in brief.

A. Blending effects associated with layers can be used to combine channels of images with new images. Apply Image command or the Calculations command can be used. These commands offer two additional blending modes namely Add and Subtract.

The calculation commands perform mathematical operations on the corresponding pixels of two channels and then combine the results in a single channel. Two concepts are fundamental to understanding how the calculation commands work:

➢ Each pixel in a channel has a brightness value. The Calculations and Apply Image commands manipulate these values to produce the resulting composite pixels.

➢ These commands overlay the pixels in two or more channels. Thus, the images used for calculations must have the same pixel dimensions.

Steps to apply Calculations command;

➢ Open the source image or images.
➢ Choose Image > Calculations.
➢ To preview the results in the image window, select Preview.
➢ Choose the first source image, layer, and channel.
➢ To use the negative of the channel contents in the calculation, select Invert.
➢ Choose the second source image, layer, and channel, and specify options.
➢ For Blending, choose a blending mode.
➢ Enter an Opacity value to specify the effect's strength.
➢ If you want to apply the blending through a mask, select Mask.
➢ Then choose the image and layer containing the mask.
➢ Specify whether to place the blending results in a new document or in a new channel or selection in the active image.

Q50.   What is match color in adjustment?

A. Match Color command matches colors between multiple images, between multiple layers, or between multiple selections. It also adjusts the colors in an image by changing the luminance, changing the color range, and neutralizing a color cast. The Match Color command works only in RGB mode. The Match Color command matches the colors in one image (the source image) with colors in another image (the target image). Match Color is useful when you're trying to make the colors in different photos consistent, or when certain colors (such as skin tones) in one image must match the colors in another image. In addition to matching the color between two images, the Match Color command can match the color between different layers in the same image.

Steps to match the color between two images

➢ Make a selection in the source and target images.
➢ Make the image that you want to change active, and then choose Image > Adjustments > Match Color.
➢ From the Source menu in the Image Statistics area of the Match Color dialog box, choose the source image whose colors you'll be matching in the target image.
➢ If you made a selection in the image, do one or more of the following:
  ▪ In the Destination Image area, select Ignore Selection When Applying Adjustment if you're applying the adjustment to the entire target image.
  ▪ In the Image Statistics area, select Use Selection In Source To Calculate Colors if you made a selection in the source image.
  ▪ In the Image Statistics area, select Use Selection In Target To Calculate Adjustment if you made a selection in the target image.
➢ To automatically remove a color cast in the target image, select the Neutralize option.
➢ To increase or decrease the brightness in the target image, move the Luminance slider.
➢ To adjust the color saturation in the target image, adjust the Color Intensity slider.
➢ To control the amount of adjustment, move the Fade slider.
➢ Click OK.

Bibliography

http://www.dummies.com
https://helpx.adobe.com/in/illustrator/
https://helpx.adobe.com/photoshop/
https://www.photoshopessentials.com/
http://www.photoshopbuzz.com
https://ipfs.io/
http://www.unipune.ac.in/
http://www.gujaratuniversity.ac.in/
http://adypu.edu.in
https://www.poornima.edu.in
https://www.sharda.ac.in
https://www.ycmou.ac.in
https://www.jainuniversity.ac.in

www.ingramcontent.com/pod-product-compliance
Lightning Source LLC
Chambersburg PA
CBHW071241240726
48654CB00009B/1149